Military Aircraft Library
Anti-Submarine Warfare

Military Aircraft Library
Anti-Submarine Warfare

DR. DAVID BAKER

Rourke Enterprises, Inc.
Vero Beach, FL 32964

Library of Congress Cataloging-in-Publication Data

Baker, David, 1944-
    Anti-submarine warfare/by David Baker.

    p. cm. — (The Military aircraft series)
    Includes index.
    Summary: Describes the goals, techniques, and specific types of planes used in anti-submarine warfare waged from the air.
    ISBN 0-86592-532-1
    1. Anti-submarine warfare — Juvenile literature
2. Anti-submarine aircraft — United States — Juvenile literature. 3. United States Navy — Juvenile literature.
[1. Anti-submarine warfare. 2. Anti-submarine aircraft.
3. Airplanes, Military.]
I. Title. II. Series: Baker, David, 1944-   Military
aircraft Library.
V214.B35   1989   88-13770
358.4'14 — dc19   CIP
                                          AC

CONTENTS

The Threat

Japanese aircraft, brought several thousand miles from their bases across the Pacific Ocean, attacked U.S. naval forces at Pearl Harbor with bombs and torpedoes.

Submarines pose one of the greatest threats to surface ships because they are able to strike without being seen and can hide in the world's oceans undetected for long periods. The submarine has been one of the most effective warships in two world wars. In World War One (1914-1918), the submarine was being used operationally for the first time in a major conflict. During World War Two (1939-1945), the submarine came of age and was used with staggering effect.

Alone in its stand against Germany between 1940 and 1942, Great Britain was blockaded by German submarines, called *U-boats* from the German word

Unterseeboote (under-sea boats). U-boats roamed the Atlantic Ocean and caused havoc among merchant ships trying to get through with food and supplies to Britain. The British have always been a seafaring nation, because as an island they were often threatened by other European countries. Now, a major power in Europe had a tool with which it

Bombs and air-dropped torpedoes were largely responsible for the devastating loss of U.S. naval forces at Pearl Harbor.

A surprise Japanese attack on Pearl Harbor in December 1941 brought the United States into World War Two.

hoped to strangle the life out of Britain and her people.

The United States responded to Great Britain's need by providing aid and a continual supply of ships and provisions. This enabled Britain to pull through until the U.S. itself entered the war against Germany, just after the Japanese attacked Pearl Harbor in December 1941. The United States, more self-sufficient than Britain, did not have to get its food from abroad. Yet the submarine threat was just as serious for America.

America was fighting the Japanese across many islands in the Pacific Ocean, and the marines who recaptured these places one by one could be supplied at first only by sea. Large numbers of merchant ships and naval vessels sailed back and forth between the United States and the Pacific islands. Japanese submarines were a serious threat at all times, and military chiefs soon acquired a healthy respect for the under-sea boat.

After the war, the United States developed several anti-submarine techniques and began to look at how aircraft could be used to fight these sub-surface threats. Meanwhile, the Soviet Union had built up strong military forces in eastern Europe and threatened to invade West European countries such as France, West Germany, and Italy. The Soviets had already taken over several East European countries,

Today, ships at sea are vulnerable to the wide-scale deployment of large submarine fleets that can inflict the kind of damage shown in this picture.

Although usually laid by surface ships, mines can also be deployed by submarines, which are more difficult to detect.

These contact mines were discovered on the deck of an Iranian ship in the Persian Gulf.

and many people thought renewed fighting was likely.

Because of this, increasing emphasis on a powerful Soviet submarine fleet worried military officials. The Soviets created a fleet of more than 300 such boats; they threatened, by their sheer presence, to create havoc on a grander scale than the U-boats had accomplished in World War Two. The German U-boat menace had been bad enough. At one point in 1943, the Germans were sinking British cargo ships faster than their replacements could be launched.

Submarines pose many new threats today. Technology has progressed to levels undreamed of a few years ago. Submarines have always threatened surface ships, but the new generation of weapons carried by these under-sea boats makes that threat more powerful than ever. Using special self-contained guidance systems, attack submarines can

now fire at and destroy targets on the surface, under the sea, or on land several hundred miles away.

Improvements in operating techniques are made possible because of *nuclear power plants*, which permit submarines to remain underwater a lot longer than their World War Two ancestors. When powered by diesel engines, oil was an essential part of keeping the submarine fleet at sea, and each submarine had to return to the surface frequently to take on extra fuel. Now, with nuclear-powered turbine engines, they can remain submerged for several weeks, or months if necessary.

Improvements in hull design and assembly have

Helicopters are a vital part of anti-submarine warfare, being capable of hovering for lengthy periods at sea and attacking submarines when contact is made.

made these boats a lot quieter underwater, even when running at speed. General improvements to the basic engineering have provided the submarine with a speed far faster than that of the surface ships that hunt them. A modern Soviet nuclear-powered hunter-killer submarine can easily accelerate to more than 40 *knots* and outrun any surface ship around. This makes them a very formidable foe, because they can hide more easily and better than ever before.

Submarines are an awesome threat for another

Naval warships are a prime target for enemy submarines because they carry offensive forces like this AH-1 Sea Cobra armed helicopter, used to back up marine operations on land.

reason. They carry a major stock of the world's most powerful nuclear weapons, and the hidden recesses of the world's oceans have become the hiding place for *ballistic-missile submarines*. In a time of international crisis, submarines of this type lie quite still and are hidden far away from their targets. If nuclear war ever broke out, they would unleash their weapons on unsuspecting civilians several thousand miles away.

The most modern ballistic-missile submarines carry between 20 and 24 such weapons. Each has greater explosive power than all the bombs and explosives used in the two world wars. This is why the submarine threat has taken on a completely new dimension from that which existed even 30 years ago. It is why the air and naval forces of all the major nations consider anti-submarine warfare, or *ASW*, to

be a vital part of national defense. Today the submarine can not only starve island countries into submission, but it can also threaten annihilation of large numbers of its population.

Military aircraft and helicopters operated by the U.S. Air Force and the U.S. Navy all play a part in building an anti-submarine screen. Planes work in cooperation with automatic sensors laid on the seabed and with robot monitoring platforms floating in the ocean. Anti-submarine warfare is a coordinated activity involving military operations under the sea, on the surface, and in the air. A large number of submarines exist to do nothing other than search, locate, identify, and destroy enemy submarines that threaten surface ships.

The United States ballistic-missile submarine USS Nathan Hale *heads for the open sea and its secret destination.*

In addition to all the technological improvements made to submarines, one other fact makes them an even greater threat. They are capable of destroying aircraft carriers quite easily. These giant ships are a powerful tool for defense, and the U.S. has only 15 of them in service. If a submarine were to destroy significant numbers of these valued warships, the nation's ability to defend itself would be crippled. That is why the ASW forces use the most modern equipment available.

Seas and Oceans

The oceans of the world are big — so big, in fact, that they are difficult to imagine on any scale. Statistics fail to give a true impression of the amount of water on the planet. The surface of the earth covers almost 200 million square miles, and the oceans account for 140 million square miles of it. Moreover, the average depth is about 12,000 feet. Altogether, that adds up to a lot of water in which submarines can hide.

Compared to land, scientists know very little about the sea. There are still many surprises. Research institutes around the world have spent much time and effort trying to discover more about the sea and its teeming life forms. Military organizations use data from these institutions to find

Merchant shipping is a vital part of international trade and nations are easily held hostage to threats of attack upon their vital economic resources.

out ways of using the seas and the oceans for defense purposes. A good understanding of the sea is an essential first step in searching for and detecting submarines.

The seas and oceans are virtually opaque to everything but sound. The exact speed of sound in water depends on a combination of things, including temperature, pressure, and the amount of salt contained in the water. Seawater consists of an average 30.6 percent sodium chloride (salt),

14

Connected to its parent ship by a wire control system, this (yellow) remotely operated vehicle moves ahead of the tanker and its escorting destroyer, searching for under-sea threats like submarines and mines.

Underwater mines are sometimes disguised to look like pieces of old wreckage or debris but this mine-hunting ship drags a special device that can detect them and warn the crew.

Vessels like this supertanker are easy targets for submarines in peace or war.

Even in peace time, commercial fleets are threatened by all manner of weapons like these mines being inspected by navy personnel in the Persian Gulf.

although the precise quantity can vary. Sound usually travels at about 3,200 MPH in water, which is 4 times faster than sound travels in air close to the ground. The speed of sound underwater is, however, affected by the levels of sodium in the water.

Concentrations of sodium and other chemicals can take place when currents come together and create violent forces. These forces create turbulent water far beneath the surface, like violent winds blowing across hills and mountains. Such forces can become so strong that they physically move submarines off course. One submarine, the USS *Thresher*, was sunk in April 1963 when it encountered severe turbulence that forced the boat down to great depths. It broke apart under stress.

Sound is a valuable tool in the search for submarines, because it travels fast and effectively.

The underwater movement of sound can be used to discover seemingly hidden objects like submarines. It does this by using the same concept as *radar*. Radar provides information about objects by sending out a radio signal that bounces off solid objects and is reflected back to the antenna that sent it. Instead of sending out a radio signal, however, *sound detectors* send a pulse of noise that is reflected from solid objects, just like radar.

Military Sealift Command has responsibility for supplying naval forces across the oceans of the world with equipment to keep watch on surface and sub-surface threats.

Complex and sophisticated radar and sonar systems combine to provide early warning of potential attack from submarine forces.

Increasing attention to underwater research means new technology is providing quieter and more efficient submarines.

Unfortunately for submarine detectors, the oceans are not simple volumes of water. They have weather just like the atmosphere does. In fact, air and water are similar in many ways, and both are fluids. Under-sea weather is difficult for us to study, but it is very real, nevertheless. In fact, the waves and tides we see on the water's surface are merely the surface effects of sometimes violent and turbulent activity far below.

One main difference between fresh water and seawater is that the oceans contain many particles of different chemicals. Scientists measure the content and record the different levels of sodium present in different waters. The term used for a change in something is *cline*. A change in sodium content is measured as *halocline*. A change in temperature is termed a *thermocline*. These changes are important for understanding how to find submarines, because equipment like sound detectors will react differently to changing conditions.

A major factor in anti-submarine warfare is the

This Mine Neutralization Vehicle is just one of a new class of vehicle designed to counter the underwater hazard.

changing temperature structure of the sea. The sun heats the top layer of the sea to a depth of about 300 feet near the poles and less than 100 feet at the equator. The temperature of the water decreases in specific layers as small as 2-4 inches. Below these is a layer where the water temperature drops sharply. This is the permanent thermocline. It is usually found at a depth of about 1,000 feet near the equator and between 1,600 feet and 3,200 feet farther away from the equator.

Just above the permanent thermocline are seasonal thermoclines that come and go at different times of the year. There are also what scientists call *diurnal thermoclines*, which appear in the morning and disappear in the afternoon. Thermoclines separate waters of slightly different densities, and particles tend to gather in these layers. These can include anything from small organisms to dissolved chemical waste from power stations and factories.

Knowledge of the changing thermoclines is important for submarine detection, because the speed of sound changes with different temperatures. It is slowest in the permanent thermocline, an area submarine hunters call the deep sound channel. Here, sound travels very far. It can travel along the channel for more than 500 miles and still have a lot of its original energy left. One

disrupting fact is that sound does not travel underwater in straight lines but in great sweeping arcs. This makes it very difficult to use sound to detect submarines.

The surfaces of the sea and the sea floor act as boundaries for these sweeping sound arcs and cause scattering and deflection of the great sound circles. The arcs converge with the reflected sound in what is called the convergence zone, leaving vast areas of the ocean unpenetrated by the transmitted sound from a submarine detector. This was not known during the early days of submarine hunting, and several ships in World War Two were sunk when U-boats got in close without being detected.

Additional complications arise from deflected sound. If a transmitter is pointed down below the horizontal in water more than 12,000 feet deep, the sound arc will bottom out in the deep sound channel

New designs of light aircraft carrier used for attacks on shore bases would be prime targets in war time.

New concepts for helicopters and vertical-launched planes would contribute to powerful new weapons systems for the war against the submarine.

and be deflected back to the surface up to 44 miles away from where it was transmitted. Surprisingly, sound levels can actually increase in the convergence zone.

Within the world's oceans are millions and billions of organisms, some extremely small. These organisms influence the way submarines can hide their presence. This life creates its own noise, adding to the underwater volcanoes, wave sounds, and the artificial sound of countless ships with rumbling engines. All this sound is scattered by what is called the deep scattering layer. It actually consists of four layers, a very thick layer and three smaller ones that contain tiny organisms called *plankton*.

The size and intensity of the layer varies with the place and the time of day. Even the thickness of the layer varies. Sound waves sent out from an underwater transmitter will not easily pass through the deep scattering layer unless the transmitter is pointing straight down. Another impediment to

sound detectors is the echo effect from solid surfaces at the bottom of the ocean. Rocks, boulders, old wrecks, and other objects all cause a scattering of reflected echoes.

Finally, tide and current also have an effect on detectors dropped in the sea, as does the weather in the earth's atmosphere. Because there is no way of knowing at what speed the detector is moving, an object that seems to be moving underwater may actually be stationary. It is the detector that is moving, not the submarine! Thunder, rain, hail, and other disturbances in the weather above the waves can affect the sounds heard through the sea. All atmospheric events influence what sound waves are sent through the water.

Planes like this are being considered for new capabilities in anti-submarine warfare.

Sub-Hunting

Submarine hunting is a fight against natural forces that all strive to deter the efforts of technicians on sea and in air. In fact, because of the complexity of sub-hunting, sea and air forces cooperate together probably more so than in any other venture that concerns the two services.

An aircraft can do much that ships are unable to accomplish. Planes cover large areas of the sea quickly and can observe things on the surface. They have the advantage of height and can observe ships over an increased area and spot tell-tale signs of submarines. Although detecting submarines is not an easy task, with the help of scientific instruments it is possible.

Submarines have various needs, and one of these is to come up to the surface. Once there, they can be seen from great distances, and aircraft are ideal for keeping watch across large areas of water. Also, submarines moving slowly close to the surface leave a tell-tale sign. Any object moving through the sea will displace a volume of water equal to its size. The water that is pushed aside rises to the surface and causes a recognizable increase in the height of the sea at that point. Very precise measurement of the average wave height will reveal the presence of an object moving underwater.

A helicopter positions an advanced lightweight dipping sonar in the water to detect submarines or other underwater vessels.

A U.S. Navy helicopter heads out on an anti-submarine search mission with sonar equipment and sounding devices.

Crew members of surface ships monitor sonar scanners looking for signs of intruding submarines and monitoring the progress of friendly submarines.

25

Above all, there are two very useful ways of detecting submarines from aircraft. One is to drop sound detectors, and the other is to measure disturbances in the earth's magnetic field. Sound detectors, or *sonobuoys*, are dropped from aircraft into the sea over wide areas. Sonobuoys get their name from the word *sonar*, which means "**so**und **na**vigation and **r**anging." It works in much the same manner as radar (**ra**dio **d**etection **a**nd **r**anging) but sends sound pulses rather than radio waves.

Reflected sounds from submarines in the sea are picked up by these sonobuoys and transmitted to the plane overhead. This information allows the plane to get a position fix on where the submarine is. It

A helicopter prepares to dangle a dipping sonar scanner in the water to report back on the possible presence of enemy submarines.

does this by comparing several sonobuoy reports together and calculating the approximate location. These *active sonar*, as they are called, send signals that can be varied according to conditions in the water.

The duration of the sound pulse and the frequency, or pitch, of the sound can be changed to give the detector the best possible conditions for picking up reflected sound from metal submarine hulls. One complication is that the movement of water around the sonobuoy will distort the signal going out and the reflection coming back. The greatest handicap, however, comes from the difficult listening conditions in different sea and ocean conditions. Planes carry several different sonobuoys suited to specific conditions.

The torpedo is the primary anti-submarine weapon and recent technology has improved the capability of these pilotless bombs.

Sonobuoys are dropped from a height of between 100 feet and 500 feet, although most can survive a drop from up to 40,000 feet. They descend on parachutes, which help to break their impact with the water. Power to operate the sonar transmitter and the signal that will be sent back to the plane comes from a battery, which is switched on by contact with seawater. The sonobuoy releases a special float that keeps one part of the device on the water as it lowers the transmitter and microphone. This end of the sonobuoy can operate from a depth of up to 1,000 feet.

Because sonobuoys are designed for different sea conditions, the aircraft may first want to find out what the temperature and sound properties are

Torpedoes are highly complex and sophisticated weapons systems that require much care and attention during manufacture and assembly.

The Spearfish torpedo is one of the most modern and effective available to naval forces today.

Because torpedoes carry out sophisticated control maneuvers in response to signals that pick up the presence of enemy submarines, their manufacture is highly precise and calls for great skill and accuracy.

before dropping its detectors. It does this by receiving information from instruments that provide details about those conditions. The pilot can then select the most appropriate sonobuoy for the sea conditions reported. This probe device is called a "bathygraph/sound velocity profiling system" and is usually deployed by surface ships. A long line is unwound to take soundings at various depths.

The other method of detecting the presence of submarines using long-range planes is the measurement of changes in the magnetic field of the earth's surface under the ocean floor. As the metal hull of a submarine passes through the earth's natural lines of magnetic force, it disturbs it. The disturbance can be measured using what is called a "magnetic anomaly detector," or *MAD*. This takes the form of a long boom out the back of the aircraft that picks up these disturbances, or anomalies.

Submarines also create electrical fields as they move. Various chemicals on the hull of the submarine generate different electrical energies that use seawater as the conductor. Some Soviet scientists believe they can detect submarines by placing large coils of wire on the sea floor. The coils

Torpedoes are not only used by submarines attacking other submarines but are also dropped by helicopters.

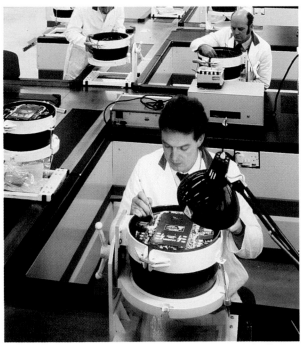

would detect the change in the electrical potential of the seawater as the submarine moved near.

Cooperation between air and sea forces is vital to get the best combination of equipment and to achieve the best anti-submarine results. Vast areas of the world's oceans are monitored for submarine activity, and the distribution of the continents brings rewards as well as penalties. One advantage of the location of different land masses is that there are certain spots submarines have to pass to get to the

Underwater warfare systems are a vital part of protecting the nation's sea lanes and insuring against surprise attack by underwater forces.

open sea. One such area is the North Atlantic, where very special preparations have been made to monitor Soviet submarines.

In what is called the "sound surveillance system," or *SOSUS*, the United States has the means to count Soviet submarines gong in and out of the Baltic Sea where big submarines are located. The U.S. has laid several hundred miles of sound detectors along the sea floor to listen for the movement of submarines. The sound detectors are called *hydrophones*. They do not send out signals to watch for reflections off solid surfaces. They are underwater ears, listening for the sound of submarines.

Submarines generate noise from their engines, from their rotating propellers, and from their movement through the water. Each sound has a characteristic tone, and sound detectors can distinguish between the sound made by different types of submarine. SOSUS works well in relatively narrow channels of water but cannot easily be used in the open sea. Too many hydrophones would be

In the immediate vicinity of the battle group, carrier forces are protected by helicopters that regularly patrol the seas with sonar devices, looking for signs of enemy attack.

The torpedo-armed submarine becomes a fully independent anti-ship warfare system, capable of operating without control from ship or shore bases.

needed to deploy them effectively in large areas of water.

Ideally, the United States would like to know where every Soviet submarine is at any particular time. This is impossible, so the next best thing is to know when submarines are in the open sea, moving to take up station somewhere, or at home in port. SOSUS hydrophones cover the sea floor in long strings of detectors spaced at specific intervals. They cover the northern approaches to the North Atlantic, where Soviet submarines must pass in order to reach open seas.

One SOSUS string stretches from Scotland to Iceland, and another goes from Iceland to Greenland. Other SOSUS hydrophones are laid down on the sea floor just north of Norway. Soviet submarines pass this spot going in or out of their northern bases. Because friendly submarine movements are known, Soviet submarines are clocked moving through these hydrophone zones to provide information about fleet movements underwater.

This information is used by land-based aircraft to patrol the seas in case of war. These planes can respond to reports coming from the SOSUS line and move to where the submarines are making a dash for the open ocean. Once through, they cannot easily be found. In wartime, the gap between Scotland and

A Sikorsky Sea Dragon trails an anti-magnetic mine detector, looking for the hidden underwater threat to shipping.

Greenland would be full of Soviet submarines trying to get out.

For a time, land-based *anti-submarine planes* were thought to be outdated by improvements in submarine technology that permitted submarines to move more quickly, quietly, and with less time on the surface. Laying down SOSUS lines all over the world in places where potentially hostile submarines pass has revolutionized anti-submarine warfare from the air. Surface ships are too restricted by their lack of speed to have the advantage planes have in the air.

Not only can they respond to SOSUS information, they can deploy and monitor sonobuoy soundings and move quickly to react to surface sightings or reports from surface ships about enemy submarines. They also carry a heavy load of anti-submarine weapons to destroy the submarines. The need to remain airborne for long periods searching oceans and watching for submarines requires a certain kind of plane.

Without helicopters the anti-submarine war would be less effective, and large, expensive ships like aircraft carriers would become much more vulnerable.

The Planes

One of the most outstanding anti-submarine planes in use today is the Lockheed P-3 Orion. It was developed in the late 1950s from a need to replace its predecessor, also built by Lockheed and called the P-2 Neptune. The Orion was essentially a converted and reworked design of the Lockheed Electra airliner, which first flew in 1957. It incorporated some very fundamental developments in data handling on anti-submarine planes. The first Orion flew in 1958 and it reached operational navy units in 1969.

Today, Orion is the U.S. Navy's most prolific land-based ASW plane. Almost 400 are still on duty, and they will remain a vital part of the navy's ASW program for a long time to come. Several versions have been produced and are continually being

The forerunner of Britain's maritime reconnaissance Shackleton was this Lancaster bomber of World War Two, modified for a maritime surveillance role.

updated with the latest electronic equipment. Some foreign air forces have purchased the P-3 for their own use as a sub-hunter, and the aircraft is still in production for the U.S. Navy as well as a range of overseas customers.

The P-3 Orion is 116 feet, 10 inches long and has a wing span of 99 feet, 8 inches and a height of 33 feet, 8 inches. Most of its ten crew members are employed operating the complex electronic equipment. Orion has an empty weight of 30 tons and maximum loaded weight of 71 tons. It is

The Shackleton was used by Britain for many years as an anti-submarine plane capable of flying many thousands of miles non-stop.

The Shackleton was gradually replaced by the Nimrod, which has been routinely patrolling the Atlantic Ocean for many years; it is a developed version of the world's first jet airliner, the Comet.

One of the most valuable anti-submarine warfare planes in use with the navy today is the Lockheed S-3A Viking carrier-based plane, first introduced during 1974.

powered by four very reliable Allison *turboprop engines*, each delivering 4,900 horsepower.

The first version of the Orion could deploy and monitor four sonobuoys, and the next version could use eight. The latest version can operate with 16 sonobuoys simultaneously. This greatly increases the ability of the technical teams aboard the plane to handle the large quantities of information broadcast by the small echo sounders to the plane in the air. The first Orion had nine sonobuoy launch chutes under the fuselage, while the latest has 48 chutes that are loaded externally.

If the Orion detects and locates the position of an enemy submarine, it can attack it with any one of a wide range of ASW weapons. These include missiles, torpedoes, rockets, depth bombs, or mines. Guided missiles include Harpoon, which has a range of up to 75 miles. Orion can carry up to four torpedoes. Depth bombs are designed to explode at pre-set depths, and mines are set to go off when a submarine passes close by. The plane can carry a total weapon load weighing almost 10 tons in an internal bay and up to ten underwing and under-fuselage pylons.

Orion has a range of almost 5,200 miles and a cruising speed of 380 MPH. The plane can fly 1,550 miles and spend three hours on patrol at its destination before turning home. On patrol it would usually fly at a height of 1,500 feet and a speed of about 240 MPH. Maximum patrol endurance on efficient fuel settings is about 16 hours.

Great Britain's Royal Air Force also includes ASW planes. The British Shackleton was built originally by the old Avro company in England. This plane is a specially designed version of the Lancaster bomber used in World War Two. The Shackleton first flew in

1949, and the Royal Air Force still operates 10 planes of this type. All of them are now used as airborne early warning planes.

The Shackleton's replacement in the sub-hunting role was the British Aerospace Nimrod, a developed version of the Comet airliner. It is the only long-range maritime aircraft to be powered by jet engines. Nimrod has a range of more than 5,000 miles and can carry a large number of weapons in addition to sonobuoys. Like the Orion, Nimrod has a magnetic anomaly detector in the tail. The plane first flew in 1967, and today the Royal Air Force operate 31.

Orion and Nimrod are land-based planes and must first fly long distances to their patrol stations.

Aircraft carriers give ASW planes a base closer to patrol zones. The Lockheed S-3 Viking is the U.S. Navy's prime carrier-based long-range ASW plane. It is 53 feet, 4 inches long and has a wing span of 68 feet, 8 inches and a height of 22 feet, 9 inches. The plane can stay in the air for 9 hours and has a top speed of 500 MPH from its twin General Electric *turbofan engines.*

The Lockheed S-3B Viking is capable of carrying missiles and other anti-submarine warfare systems.

The most effective land-based anti-submarine warfare plane flying today is the Lockheed P-3C Orion, powered by four turboprop engines and carrying a crew of ten.

The Viking is fully equipped with radar, magnetic anomaly detector, and 60 sonobuoy chutes. It can respond quickly to warnings of approaching submarines or remain on patrol for long periods playing a listening game through the sound detectors in the sea. If it does find a target, it can use torpedoes, missiles, rockets, or bombs to destroy it. The plane has underwing pylons for additional fuel in special tanks.

A typical carrier has 10 Vikings on board. As the principal long-range sub-hunters, these planes protect not only the carrier but also the battle group of other surface ships and submarines. Lockheed, P-3 Orion's builder, is the sole producer of fixed-wing ASW planes in service with the U.S. Navy. About 140 Vikings are in use. These planes are being called upon to hunt down submarines from farther and farther away. Soviet submarines armed with long-range *anti-ship missiles* can destroy planes that come within a range of several hundred miles.

At the other end of the distance range, carriers employ helicopters to patrol the local area. The U.S. Navy currently has about 100 Kamen SH-2 Seasprite, 100 Sikorsky SH-3 Sea King, and more than 80 Sikorsky SH-60 Seahawk ASW helicopters. A typical carrier would have 6 Sea Kings for anti-submarine work, while the Seasprites and the Seahawks are deployed on destroyers, cruisers, and

The Orion can carry a wide range of sophisticated observation and surveillance equipment in addition to large quantities of search stores and weapons.

Dropping flares to put anti-aircraft missiles off track, this Orion is a vital part of maintaining the freedom of the sea lanes.

On the surface or beneath the waves, submarines are vulnerable to the fire power of this benign-looking P-3.

An important tool in ship protection is the Kaman SH-2F LAMPS helicopter, which has a range of about seventy miles.

frigates. The navy intends to buy 200 Seahawks, some of which will be operated from the latest guided-missile destroyers.

One big advantage the helicopter has over fixed-wing planes is that it can remain stationary over one spot. Because of this, anti-submarine helicopters carry what is called *dipping sonar*. The helicopter hovers and lowers to the sea a sonar attached to a line on the helicopter's crane. From this the helicopter receives information fixed-wing planes would get by radio signals from floating sonobuoys. One firm advantage with this technique is that the movement of the sonar device can be controlled, whereas a free-floating sonar can drift long distances on currents. As noted earlier, this can create a false impression of a target's speed through the water.

The Seasprite has a length of 40 feet, 6 inches and a rotor diameter of 44 feet. It has a normal takeoff weight of more than 6 tons and can cruise along at 125 MPH. It has a range of almost 400 miles and has two General Electric *turboshaft engines* each of which delivers 1,350 horsepower. A variety of sonobuoys and *homing torpedoes* can be carried by this helicopter. Seasprite will remain the navy's most important ASW support helicopter until it is replaced by Seahawk.

The Seahawk is one of a successful family of Series 60 helicopters built by Sikorsky for the U.S. Air Force, Army, and Navy. The Seahawk is 50 feet long and the diameter of its rotor is 50 feet, 8 inches. Its maximum weight exceeds 11 tons. This helicopter has a top speed of 145 MPH and can stay on station for more than three hours. It is powered by

One of a new breed in the anti-submarine helicopter warfare group, this Sikorsky SH-60F makes its initial flight for tests and anti-submarine trials.

42

The SH-2 helicopter crew go through final pre-flight checks before setting off on a mission that could last everal hours, searching for potentially harmful submarines.

43

The SH-60F will be an impressive tool in the arsenal of anti-submarine equipment based on land and at sea.

Operating from the USS Deyo, *an SH-60B conducts anti-submarine warfare operations for a fast-moving battle group.*

two General Electric turboshaft engines of 1,690 horsepower, which gives it a degree of safety that single-engine helicopters do not possess.

The Seahawk operates in conjunction with the ship it is based on, and technicians aboard the ship monitor sensors it deploys for ASW work. It has a crew of three including pilot, airborne tactical officer, and sensor operator. The Seahawk carries anti-submarine weapons, but also operates in another role. It can be used to provide the ship with information about targets over the horizon and out of sight from the surface. High above the sea and some distance away, it provides data that long-range missiles launched from the ship can use to attack surface targets.

The big anti-submarine jobs for carriers are done by Sea King helicopters. The first Sea King flight was as long ago as 1959; Sea King joined the navy in 1961 and has been exported to nine countries. Sea King is 54 feet, 9 inches long, has a rotor diameter of 62 feet, and weighs a maximum 10 tons. It can land on the surface of the water, because its body is shaped like a boat. It is powered by two General Electric 1,400-horsepower turboshaft engines.

The Sea King can remain in the air for more than four hours and has a range of more than 600 miles with a top speed of 165 MPH. A total of 255 Sea King helicopters were built for the navy, and several versions have emerged over its long years of service. It has seen almost 30 years as a sub-hunter and has proved to be a reliable and valued tool for carrier battle group defense. When the time comes to retire this helicopter from service, what will replace it? Although nothing has been decided, some U.S. Navy officials have suggested an improved version of the Seahawk as a replacement.

GLOSSARY

Active sonar — Sonar devices that send signals out and receive back reflected sound from solid objects underwater.

Anti-ship missiles — Missiles fired from surface or air against ships at sea.

Anti-submarine warfare (ASW) — Warfare that involves air and naval forces in the detection and destruction of submarines.

Anti-submarine planes — Aircraft equipped to fight anti-submarine warfare by detecting the presence of enemy submarines and attacking them.

Ballistic-missile submarine — A submarine carrying powerful nuclear-tipped ballistic missiles, capable of attacking targets on land or at sea across intercontinental distances.

Cline — Used as a scientific term, cline indicates a change in the chemical composition of a fluid or a change in temperature.

Dipping sonar — A sonar device dangled in the water from a stationary anti-submarine helicopter.

Diurnal thermoclines — Changes in the temperature of water levels which occur repeatedly at the same time each day.

Halocline — Used by marine scientists to indicate a change in the amount of sodium found in water.

Homing torpedoes — Torpedoes designed to home in on the hull of a ship or submarine; they are attracted by the metal in the ship's construction or the specific sound frequency of its engine.

Hydrophones — Sound detectors, working on the sonar principle, that pick up sound underwater just like microphones pick up sound in air.

Knots — The speed of a object measured in nautical miles per hour. A nautical mile is just over 6,076 feet compared to a statute mile, which is 5,280 feet. Therefore 10 nautical MPH (knots) is equal to 11.5 statute MPH (usually expressed as 11.5 MPH).

Magnetic Anomaly Detector (MAD) — A device carried by aircraft and ships that detects a submarine by picking up the changes in the earth's magnetic field created by the submarine.

Nuclear power plants — Nuclear-powered engines that generate steam from water heated by nuclear reactors.

Plankton — Tiny micro-organisms that provide food for marine animals and that discolor and change the chemical nature of water in seas and oceans.

Radar — **Ra**dio **d**etection **an**d **r**anging. A system of detecting objects by bouncing radio signals off them.

Sound detectors — Devices designed to pick up and transmit information about sounds heard underwater.

46

Sonobuoys	Sound detectors dropped from aircraft into the sea or lowered by ships into the water.
Sonar	**So**und, **na**vigation and **r**anging, a detection technique in which sound waves are bounced off objects to determine their size, location, and shape.
Sound Surveillance System (SOSUS)	A sound surveillance system composed of numerous sound detectors laid by the United States across several hundred miles of seabed to detect the presence of submarines.
Thermocline	A change in water temperature from one level to another.
Turbofan engine	A jet engine with blades arranged in a circle like a fan to increase the amount of air delivered to the combustion chamber.
Turboprop engine	A jet engine that receives its main thrust from a turbine-driven propeller.
Turboshaft engines	The same as turboprop engine.
U-Boat	The common name given to German submarines, derived from Unterseeboot, the German word for under-sea boat.

INDEX

Page references in *italics* indicate photographs or illustrations.

OCT 2 7 1997	DATE DUE		